Norma Samuelson
a life, an orphan

Summary: Pictures tell the story of an orphan boy
who encounters difficult situations. He ends up at an
orphanage, goes to school, gets his degree as a teacher
and returns to his dear home the orphanage. The story is
based on the real life of an orphan in Mexico.

ISBN 978-1-7329192-3-5

Published by **Esperanza Press**, 2019

Norma Samuelson

a life, an orphan

With gratitude to Gabrielle Vincent for the inspiration of this book, which was based on the concept of her book *A day, a dog*

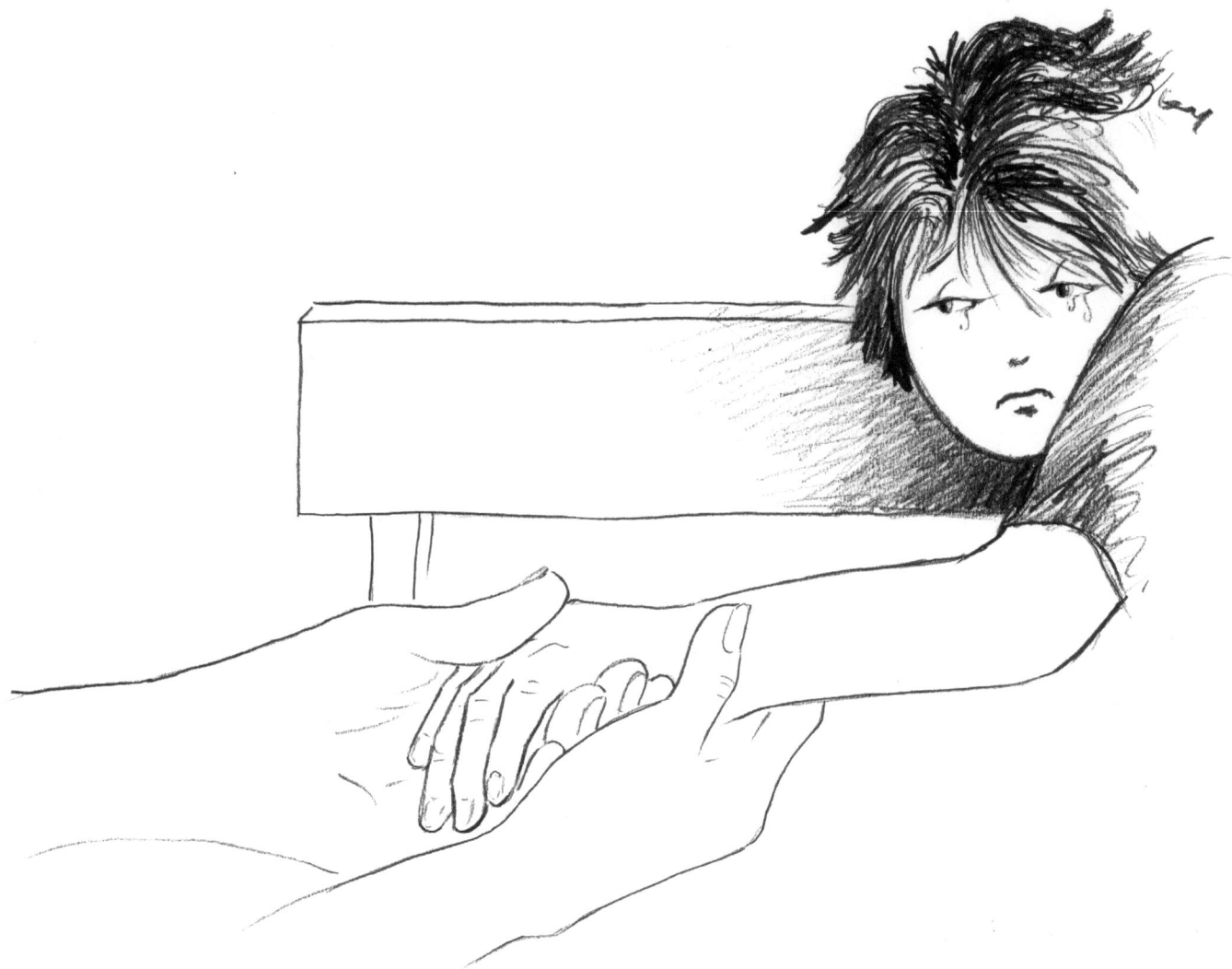

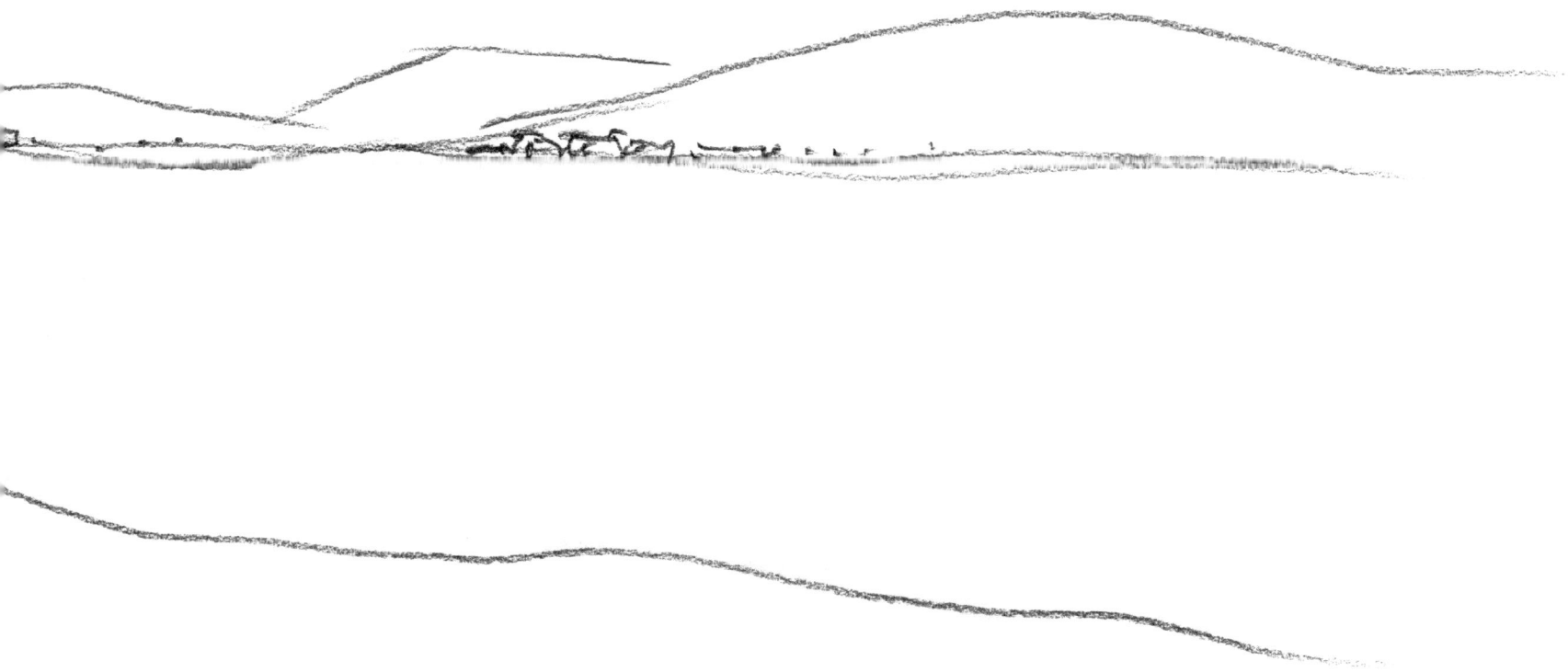

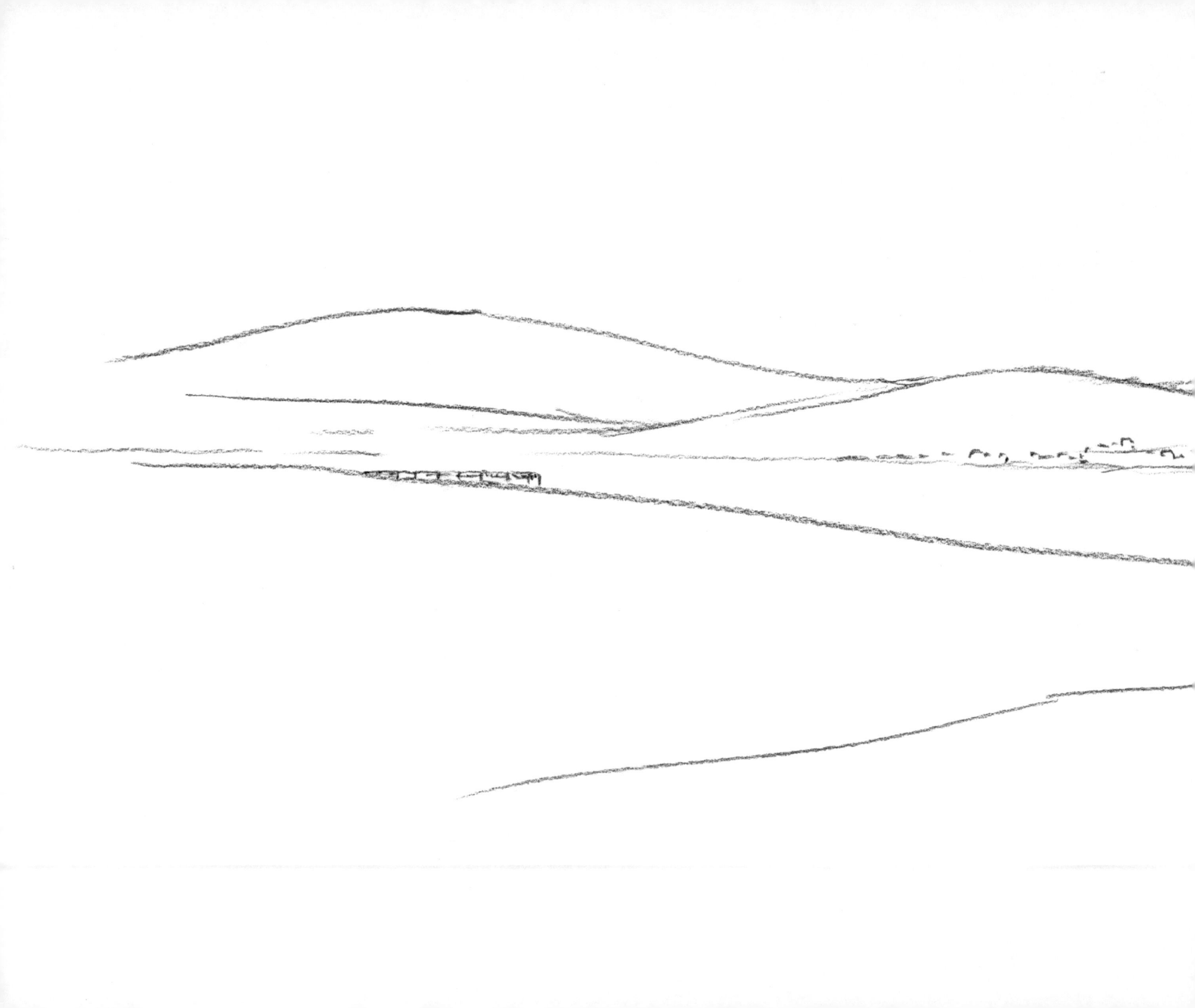

Norma Samuelson
a life, an orphan

This book uses the font 'Bell MT'

ISBN 978-1-7329192-3-5

Published by **Esperanza Press**, 2019